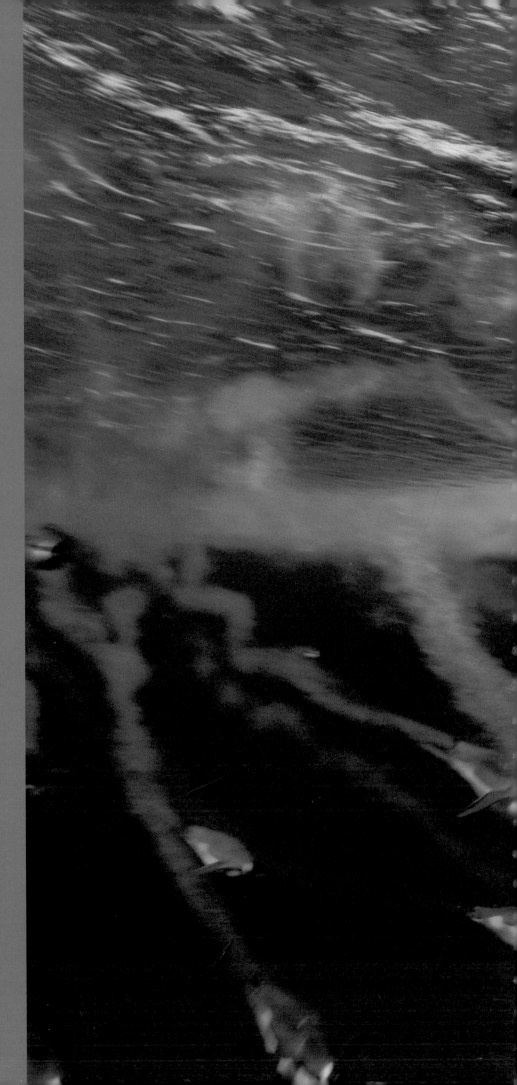

Published by Creative Education
P.O. Box 227, Mankato, Minnesota 56002
Creative Education is an imprint of
The Creative Company
www.thecreativecompany.us

Design and production by The Design Lab
Art direction by Rita Marshall
Printed by Corporate Graphics
in the United States of America

Photographs by Getty Images (Ira Block, Bill
Curtsinger, Tui De Roy, John Eastcott and Yva
Momatiuk, Darrell Gulin, Johnny Johnson, Ty Milford,
Paul Nicklen, Flip Nicklin, Joseph Van Os, Norbert
Wu), iStockphoto (Sam Lee, Jan Will)

Library of Congress Cataloging-in-Publication Data
Bodden, Valerie.
Penguins / by Valerie Bodden.
p. cm. — (Amazing animals)
Includes bibliographical references and index.
Summary: A basic exploration of the appearance,
behavior, and habitat of penguins, a family of
flightless birds. Also included is a story from folklore
explaining why emperor penguins are so big.
ISBN 978-1-58341-810-9
1. Penguins—Juvenile literature. I. Title. II. Series.
QL696.S473B63 2010
598.47—dc22   2009002712

CPSIA: 032511 PO1440
9 8 7 6 5

AMAZING ANIMALS
PENGUINS

BY VALERIE BODDEN

CREATIVE EDUCATION

Penguins are birds. But penguins cannot fly. They like to swim instead. There are 17 kinds of penguins in the world.

A penguin can swim through water as well as a fish

Most penguins have bodies that are shaped like bowling pins. They are covered with feathers. Penguins have a dark back and a light belly. Some kinds of penguins have yellow or orange feathers on their head. Penguins have short, stiff wings called flippers.

Dark backs help penguins soak up the sun's heat

Penguins come in many different sizes. Little blue penguins are the smallest penguins. They are only 16 inches (40 cm) tall. They weigh less than a newborn human baby. Emperor penguins are the biggest penguins. They can be four feet (1.2 m) tall and weigh up to 90 pounds (40 kg)!

The rockhopper penguin is a small-sized penguin

*Many penguins live on
the icy land of Antarctica*

All penguins live in the Southern Hemisphere (*HEM-is-feer*). Many penguins live on the **continent** of Antarctica. It is very cold there. Other penguins live on the continents of South America, Australia, and Africa.

Southern Hemisphere the southern, or bottom, half of Earth

continent one of Earth's seven big pieces of land

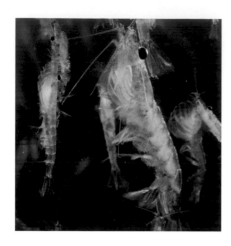

*Sometimes penguins share
food with each other*

Penguins eat food from the ocean. Many penguins eat small fish such as anchovies (*AN-cho-vees*) or sardines. Other penguins eat **krill**. Some penguins eat squid.

krill tiny water animals that look like shrimp

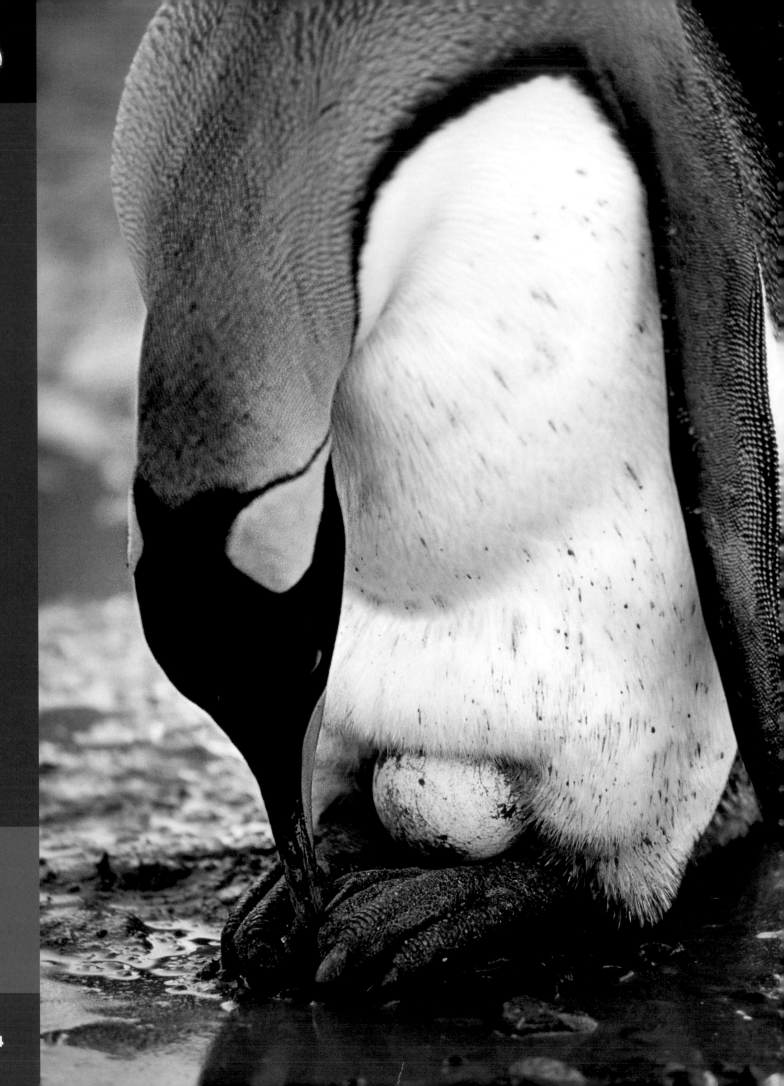

Mother and father penguins take good care of eggs

Mother penguins lay one or two eggs at a time. Mother and father penguins take turns caring for the eggs. Soon, chicks come out of the eggs. They are covered with **down**. When their grown-up feathers come in, they leave their parents. Wild penguins can live 15 to 20 years.

down soft, fluffy feathers on baby birds

Penguins spend a lot of time swimming around looking for food. They flap their flippers to move through the water. Some penguins stay in the water for many months at a time.

Penguins like to swim near other penguins

There can be thousands of penguins in some groups

When penguins are on land, they gather in big groups. The groups are noisy! Penguins can honk, squawk, and **bray**.

bray make a sound like a donkey makes

Most people do not live near penguins. But lots of people like to watch penguins in zoos. It is fun to watch them swim through the water or slide over the ice on their bellies!

Penguins can slide faster than they can walk

A Penguin Story

Why are emperor penguins so big? People in South America used to tell a story about this. They said that once there was a flood. Water covered the whole world. People had to live in the water. Some of them climbed onto big sheets of ice to live with the penguins. After a while, the people turned into penguins. They were the biggest penguins of all— emperor penguins!

Read More

Hall, Margaret. *Penguins and Their Chicks*. Mankato, Minn.: Capstone Press, 2004.

Townsend, Emily Rose. *Penguins*. Mankato, Minn.: Capstone Press, 2004.

Web Sites

Enchanted Learning: Penguins
http://www.enchantedlearning.com/subjects/birds/printouts/penguins.shtml
This site has coloring pages for many kinds of penguins.

KidZone: Penguins
http://www.kidzone.ws/animals/penguins
This site has penguin facts, activities, and photos.